GREAT CARRIER REEF

by **JESSICA STREMER**

illustrated by **GORDY WRIGHT**

holiday house • new york

Once a floating city
where sailors scurried
as planes launched into battle,
the USS *Oriskany* completed hundreds of daring missions,
earning the nickname "The Mighty O."

After years of battering by the salty sea,

the retired aircraft carrier seemed destined to sit chained to a pier.

Rusted, empty, without purpose.

But for the Mighty O,

a different fate was coming.

Beneath the waves,
thousands of marine animals use reefs
for food, shelter, and protection.

Around the world,
reefs are under attack.
Warming water temperatures, pollution, and overfishing
threaten to destroy this important ecosystem.

Unlike the Mighty O,
which survived its battles unscathed,
the future of reefs and the animals they serve
is bleak.

Off the coast of Florida,
reef fish living near a stretch of sandy ocean floor need help.
With little natural protection,
venturing into the open ocean to feed
means risking exposure
to prowling predators.

What this spot needs is something solid.
Something mighty.
Where new life can take root
and thrive.

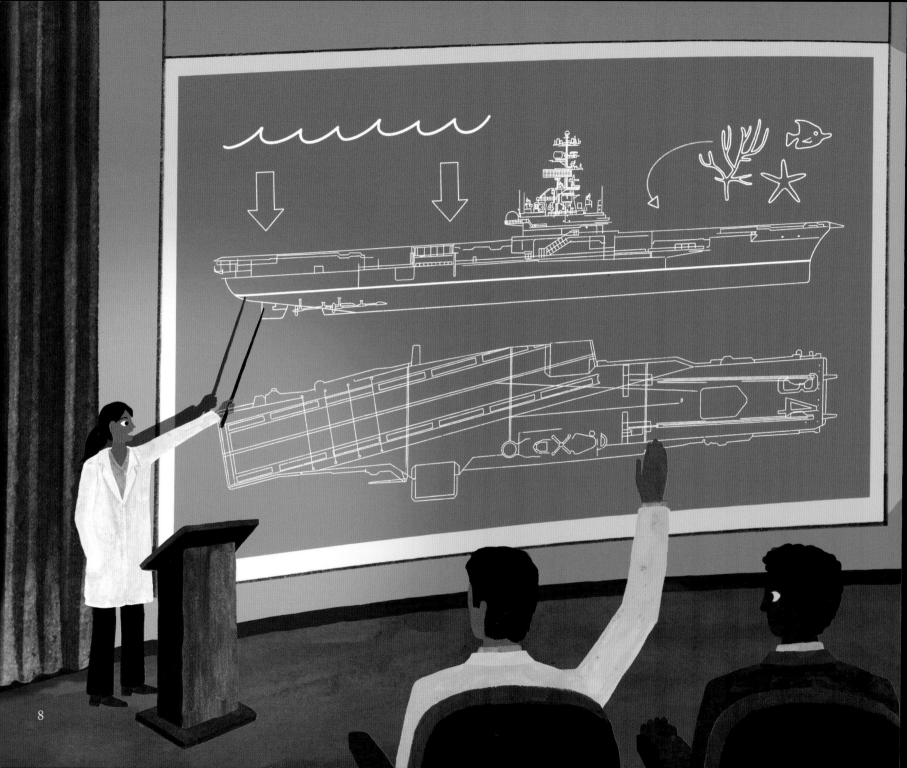

Scientists brainstorm ways to create new habitat.
They call the Mighty O out of retirement.
This time, the ship is needed on the ocean floor.
Its massive size will offer marine invertebrates, sea squirts,
and mollusks a large surface to grow on.
Hidey-holes for animals to evade predators.
And new opportunities for fishers to fish.

If successful,
the Mighty O will become the world's largest artificial reef.
But first,

a massive transformation.

Engineers march across the aircraft carrier's flight deck.

Blowtorches blaze.

Welding sparks fly.

Copper is reclaimed and sold to pay for the ship's transformation.

Oil and fuel,

poisonous to marine animals,

are drained from pipes, pumps, and tanks.

Cables and wires are severed,

the interior gutted,

toxic paint scrubbed away.

12

Layer after layer of harmful material is removed until
the Mighty O is nothing more than a shell
of its former self.

Powerless,

the Mighty O relies on tugboats to escort it over five hundred miles to Pensacola, Florida,

for the final phase of its mission.

A tug-line breaks.

Currents carry the ship dangerously close to shore.

Crews work quickly to attach a line and regain control.

The Mighty O journeys on.

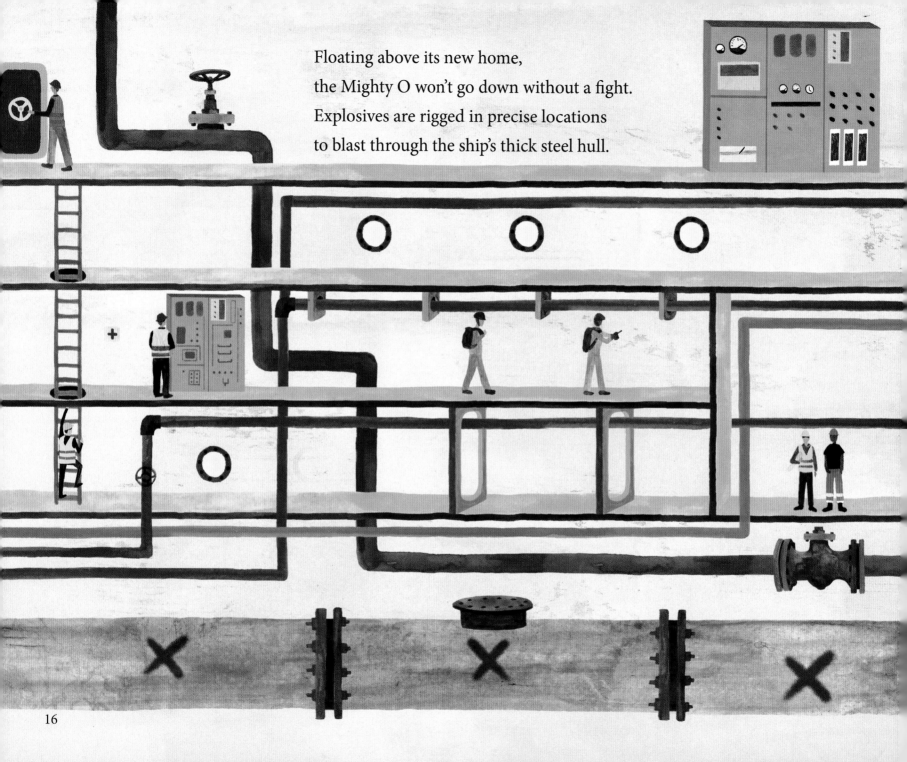

Floating above its new home,
the Mighty O won't go down without a fight.
Explosives are rigged in precise locations
to blast through the ship's thick steel hull.

One miscalculation,
one failed explosion,
could cause the ship to flood unevenly
and roll onto its side as it sinks,
leaving the ship unstable and unsafe.
Will they get it right?

KABOOM!

Water rushes through holes in the hull of the ship,
forcing air out, flooding the interior.
After more than fifty-five years above the surface,
the once unsinkable Mighty O forever disappears beneath the waves
in only thirty-seven minutes.

       But will life follow?

Hours later,
divers descend and discover . . .

24

Carried by the current,
sea squirt, mollusk, and octocoral larvae
land on the Mighty O.

All across the ship,
    new life
        attaches . . .

and

grows.

Eagle rays glide through steel
caverns. Urchins parade across
the former flight deck.
Barracuda patrol for prey
as red snapper, grouper,
and amberjack graze.

The Mighty O serves on,
solid and stationary,
transformed into
the GREAT CARRIER REEF.

REEFS

Natural reefs are made up of habitat-forming organisms such as coral, mollusks, sponges, and bryozoans (a type of aquatic invertebrate). These organisms attach themselves to submerged rocks or other hard surfaces and slowly grow together to form colonies.

Coral reefs are the most common type of natural reef habitat. Coral polyps range in size from a tiny pinhead to larger than a basketball. 'Hard' or 'hermatypic' corals produce a skeleton by excreting a material that often cements together with other hard corals to form one large reef. Many people mistake hard coral for rock. 'Soft' or 'ahermatypic' corals, such as those found on the Mighty O, do not produce a skeleton. They are more flexible and often resemble swaying plants or trees.

Though reefs cover less than 1 percent of the ocean floor, they are home to about a quarter of all fish species. Reefs also help protect coastlines from erosion, provide people with food and a source of income, and offer divers an underwater playground to explore.

Unfortunately, many reefs are dying due to disease, warming water temperatures, pollution, and overfishing.

Artificial reefs are man-made structures designed to encourage regrowth and new ecosystems. These formations increase fishing and tourist opportunities, often decreasing human activity near depleted natural reefs and thus offering those reefs time to repair.

Scientists aim to build artificial reefs on empty stretches of the ocean floor. Adding a single element, such as a sunken ship, can stimulate a dramatic change in the underwater community as the new reef becomes an oasis for fish.

MORE ABOUT THE MIGHTY O

The Mighty O remains the largest ship ever reefed. It appealed to scientists because of its massive size and solid construction. Made from durable steel, the surface of the ship provided a good structure for ahermatypic coral to grow.

A team of more than 150 people helped prepare the ship for reefing. Intentionally reefed ships are cleaned as much as possible before sinking. Even so, some harmful materials are left behind. Scientists routinely sample fish caught near artificial reefs to monitor toxicant levels.

After cleaning the Mighty O, the team used shape charges—highly focused explosives that can cut through steel—to blast through the bottom of the ship's hull. The careful placement of the charges helped minimize structural damage. If the ship had landed on its side, it would have been prone to shifting underwater during storms, making it unsafe for marine life and divers.

The team chose a sandy bottom near rock outcroppings on the ocean floor, which shortened the distance that fish would have to travel to reach food and shelter. Scientists also ensured that the location would not create a navigation hazard for large ships or interfere with gas pipelines and telecommunication cables.

Resting about twenty nautical miles off the coast of Pensacola, the Mighty O is an underwater city teeming with life. Each year the clear, warm waters attract hundreds of scuba divers who descend over 200 feet beneath the surface to explore the reef. Scientists hope the reef will continue to thrive for many years to come.

FACTS ABOUT THE USS *ORISKANY*

COMMISSIONED: SEPTEMBER 25, 1950

DECOMMISSIONED: SEPTEMBER 30, 1975

REEFED: MAY 17, 2006

DAYS IN ACTIVE SERVICE: 8,784

AIRCRAFT CAPACITY: 80–100

BATTLE STARS EARNED: 7

The USS *Oriskany* launched more aircraft and completed more missions than any other aircraft carrier of its time, earning the nickname "The Mighty O." It spent most of its time serving in the waters of the Pacific Ocean, regularly returning to the United States for maintenance and crew swaps. After twenty-five years of service, the ship was retired as an aircraft carrier. A memorial to those who perished while serving onboard the USS *Oriskany* is located at Trinkaus Park in Oriskany, New York.

U.S. Navy National Museum of Naval Aviation

The U.S. Navy aircraft carrier USS *Oriskany* (CVA-34) underway near Midway Atoll in 1967.

SELECT SOURCES

"Aircraft Carrier Photo Index: USS ORISKANY (CV-34)." NavSource Online: Aircraft Carrier Photo Archive. Accessed March 17, 2021. https://www.navsource.org/archives/02/34.htm.

"Artificial Reef." ScienceDirect. Accessed May 4, 2021. https://www.sciencedirect.com/topics/earth-and-planetary-sciences/artificial-reef.

"Coral Reproduction 101: A Crash Course in How Coral Multiplies." Seattle Aquarium. Accessed May 6, 2021. https://www.seattleaquarium.org/blog/coral-reproduction-101-crash-course-how-coral-multiplies.

"Escambia County Artificial Reef Plan (v.2009.1)." Escambia County Marine Resources Division, January 26, 2009. https://myescambia.com/docs/default-source/sharepoint-natural-resources-management/Marine%20Resources/Personal%20Reefs/20090126esccoartreefplan.pdf?sfvrsn=11.

Gabriel, Melissa Nelson. "Oriskany: 10 Years as 'The Great Carrier Reef.'" *Pensacola News Journal*, May 16, 2016. https://www.pnj.com/story/news/local/2016/04/24/10-years-later-orkisany-reef-international-dive-destination/82957574/.

Martin, Amanda. "USS ORISKANY ARTIFICIAL REEF."
Mission Resolve, September 16, 2019.
https://missionresolve.org/uss-oriskany-artificial-reef/.

"Oriskany (CV-34)." Naval History and Heritage Command. Accessed May 4, 2021.
https://www.history.navy.mil/research/histories/ship-histories/danfs/o/oriskany.html.

"Progress report summarizing the reef fish sampling, PCB analysis results and visual
monitoring associated with the Oriskany Reef, a decommissioned former Navy aircraft
carrier sunk in 2006 as an artificial reef in the Northeastern Gulf of Mexico off Pensacola,
Florida." Florida Fish and Wildlife Conservation Commission, April 13, 2011.
https://earthjustice.org/sites/default/files/Oriskany-Reef-PCB-Monitoring.pdf.

The Sinking Of An Aircraft Carrier | USS Oriskany | Spark. YouTube, 2020.
https://www.youtube.com/watch?v=F2-Aew7SMO8.

U.S. Department of Commerce, National Oceanic and Atmospheric Administration.
"Coral Reefs." NOAA's National Ocean Service, June 10, 2016.
https://oceanservice.noaa.gov/ocean/corals/.

"USS Oriskany." H2O Below, March 10, 2021.
https://ussoriskanydiver.com/services/uss-oriskany/.

YOU CAN HELP SAVE OUR REEFS!

• Bring an empty container to gather trash left on the beach.

• Wear sunscreen that is designated safe for reefs.

• Leave only footprints on the sand and bubbles in the water!

• Don't buy jewelry or other items made from corals.

• Write a letter to your legislators asking them to support reef restoration.

INDEX

SPECIAL THANKS

A wave of gratitude goes out to Captain Robert Turpin, Escambia County Marine Resources Manager; Keith Mille, Florida FWC Artificial Reef Program; Jon Dodrill, Marine Fisheries Biological Administrator, Florida FWC (retired); and Todd Schauer, Resolve Marine, for their help in reviewing the accuracy of this book. For those who served aboard the USS *Oriskany* and their families, thank you.

Amar and Isabelle Guillen - Guillen Photo LLC / Alamy Stock Photo

Oriskany wreck sunk off Pensacola, Florida

For my anchor, MDS –J. S.
For my Claremont crewmates –G. W.

A Books for a Better Earth™ Title

The Books for a Better Earth™ collection is designed to inspire young people to become active, knowledgeable participants in caring for the planet they live on. Focusing on solutions to climate change challenges and human environmental impacts, the collection looks at how scientists, activists, and young leaders are working to safeguard Earth's future.

Library of Congress Cataloging-in-Publication Data

Names: Stremer, Jessica, author. | Wright, Gordy, illustrator.
Title: Great Carrier Reef / by Jessica Stremer ; illustrated by Gordy Wright.
Description: First edition. | New York : Holiday House, [2023] | Series:
Books for a better earth | Includes bibliographical references and index. | Audience: Ages 4–8 | Audience: Grades K–1
Summary: "A STEM picture book documenting the transformation of an aircraft carrier that was gutted and turned into the world's largest artificial reef" –Provided by publisher. | Identifiers: LCCN 2022030000 | ISBN 9780823452682 (hardcover)
Subjects: LCSH: Oriskany Reef (Fla.)–History–Juvenile literature. | Oriskany (Aircraft carrier : CVA 34)–History–Juvenile literature. | Artificial reefs–Florida–Juvenile literature.
Classification: LCC SH157.85.A7 S77 2023 | DDC 551.42/4–dc23/eng/20220712
LC record available at https://lccn.loc.gov/2022030000

ISBN: 978-0-8234-5268-2 (hardcover)
ISBN: 978-0-8234-5877-6 (paperback)